JOSEPH MIDTHUN   SAMUEL HITI

BUILDING BLOCKS of SCIENCE

FIGHTING SICKNESS

WORLD
BOOK

a Scott Fetzer company
Chicago
www.worldbook.com

World Book, Inc.
233 N. Michigan Avenue
Chicago, IL 60601
U.S.A.

For information about other World Book publications,
visit our website at www.worldbook.com
or call 1-800-WORLDBK (967-5325).
For information about sales to schools and libraries,
call 1-800-975-3250 (United States),
or 1-800-837-5365 (Canada).

Library of Congress Cataloging-in-Publication Data

Fighting sickness.
    pages cm. -- (Building blocks of science)
  Summary: "A graphic nonfiction volume that
introduces the human body's immune response to
infectious disease"-- Provided by publisher.
  Includes index.
  ISBN 978-0-7166-1845-4
  1. Immunology--Juvenile literature. 2. Immune
system--Juvenile literature. 3. Communicable
diseases--Immunological aspects--Juvenile
literature. I. World Book, Inc.
QR181.8.F54 2014
616.07'9--dc23
                        2013023498

Building Blocks of Science
ISBN: 978-0-7166-1840-9 (set, hc.)

Printed in China by Shenzhen Donnelley
Printing Co., Ltd., Guangdong Province
1st printing October 2013

Acknowledgments:
Created by Samuel Hiti and Joseph Midthun
Art by Samuel Hiti
Written by Joseph Midthun
Special thanks to Syril McNally

TABLE OF CONTENTS

There is a glossary on page 30. Terms defined in the glossary are in type **that looks like this** on their first appearance.

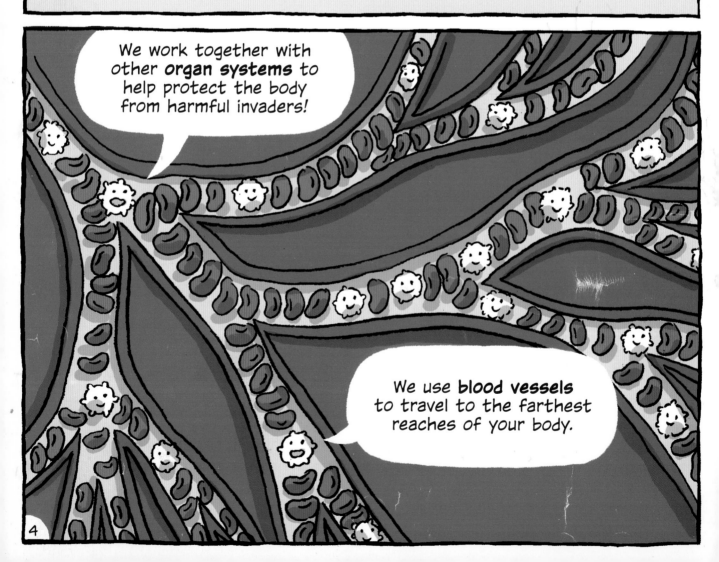

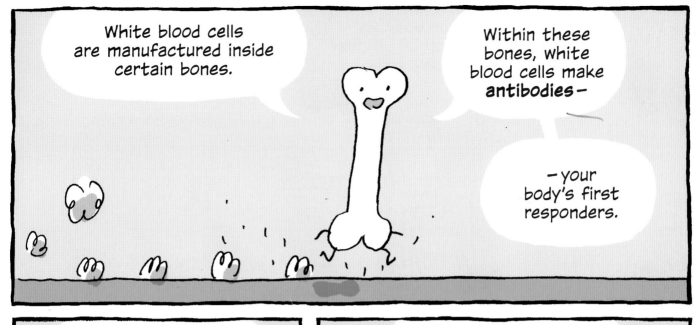

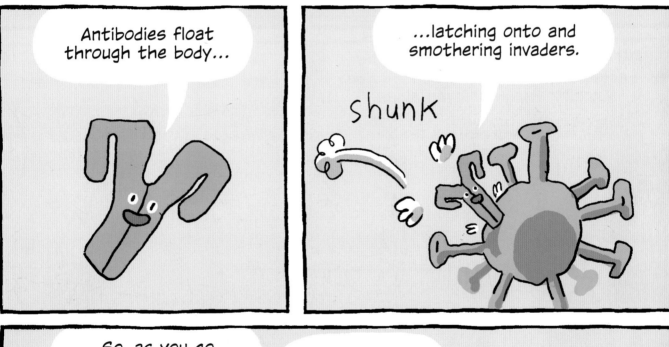

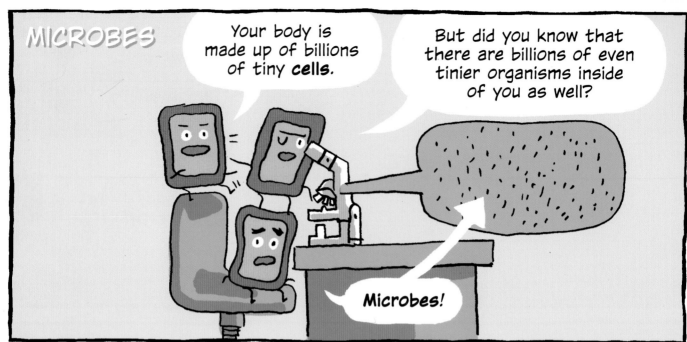

Your body is made up of billions of tiny **cells.**

But did you know that there are billions of even tinier organisms inside of you as well?

Microbes!

Microbes in your body are mostly **bacteria**, but microbes can also be **viruses**, **fungi**, or even **algae.**

Most microbes in your body are much smaller than cells.

In fact, the bacteria in your intestines are so small they outnumber the rest of the cells in your entire body.

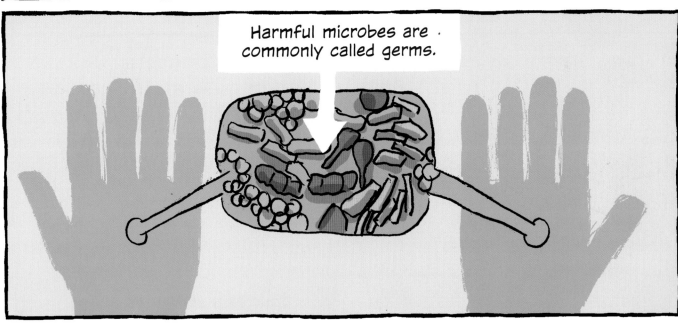

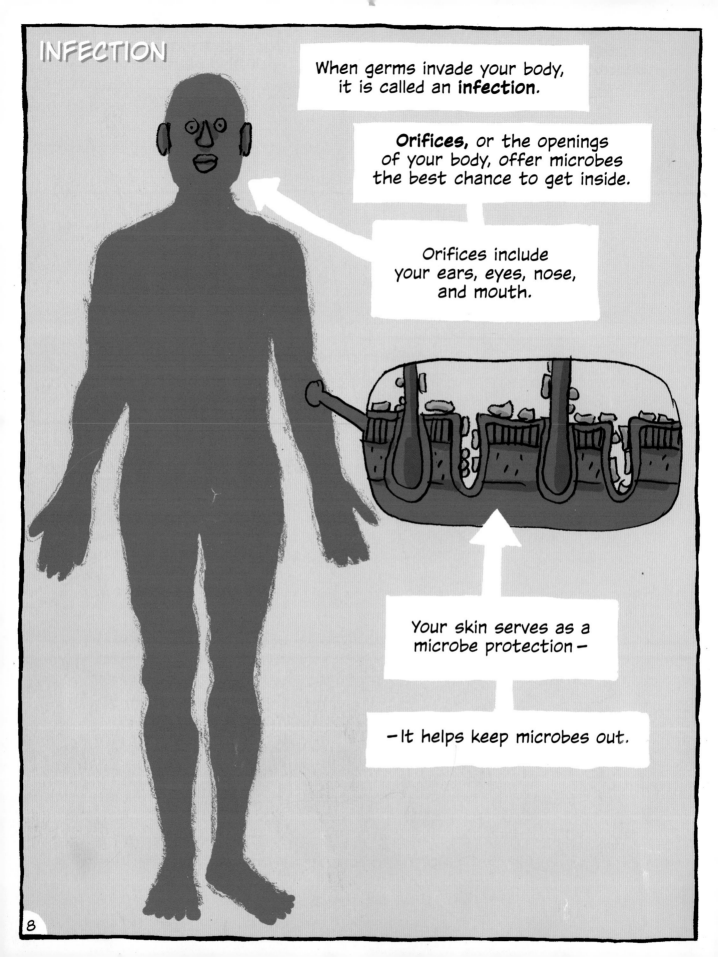

If you get a cut or a scrape, it acts like an open door, inviting germs inside.

Once inside, an infection can fester...

...or the germs can spread to other parts of the body.

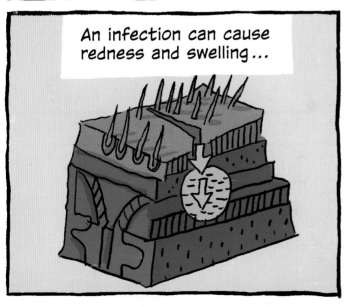

An infection can cause redness and swelling...

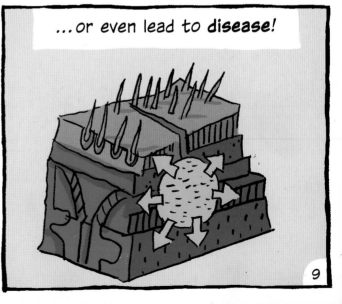

...or even lead to **disease**!

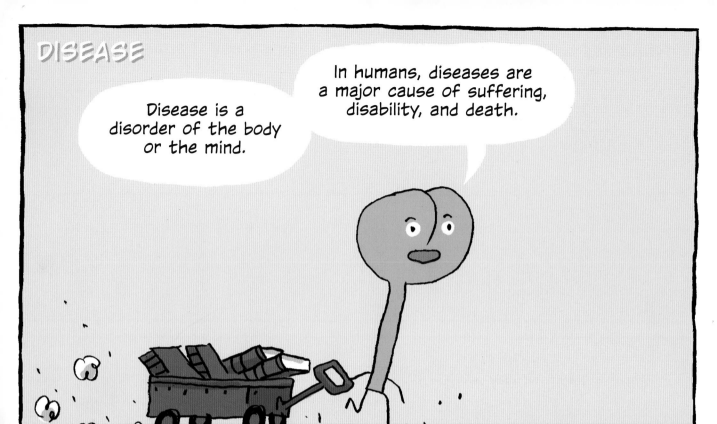

Plague and tuberculosis are deadly diseases caused by bacteria.

Smallpox and measles are the result of tiny viruses.

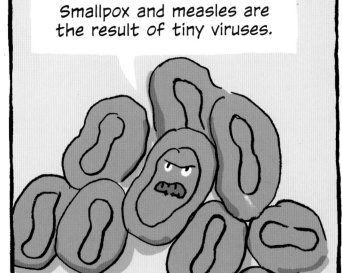

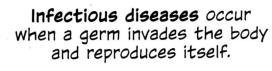 **Infectious diseases** occur when a germ invades the body and reproduces itself.

Some infectious diseases can be mild, such as a cold.

Others can be life-threatening!

Many infectious diseases easily spread from person to person.

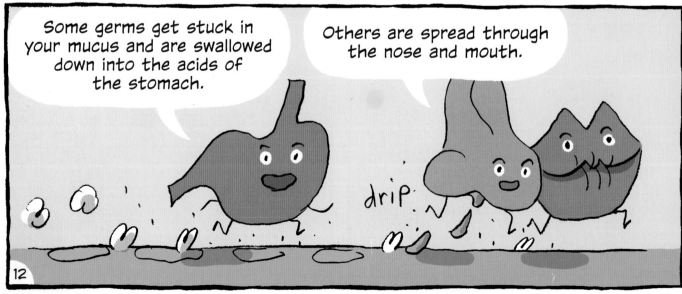

The force of a sneeze or cough ejects a mist of tiny particles of mucus out of the nose and mouth...

...into the air!

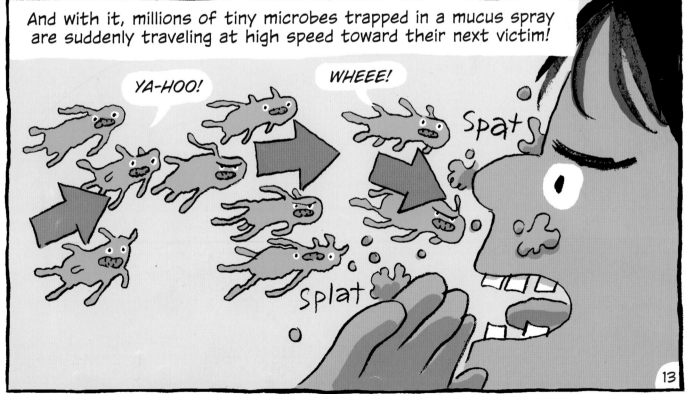

And with it, millions of tiny microbes trapped in a mucus spray are suddenly traveling at high speed toward their next victim!

Diseases can spread in other ways, too.

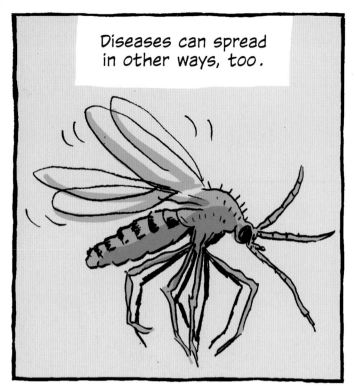

Some diseases are caused by **vectors,** also known as carriers of infectious disease.

Insects and other animals can act as vectors.

They can infect anything they bite.

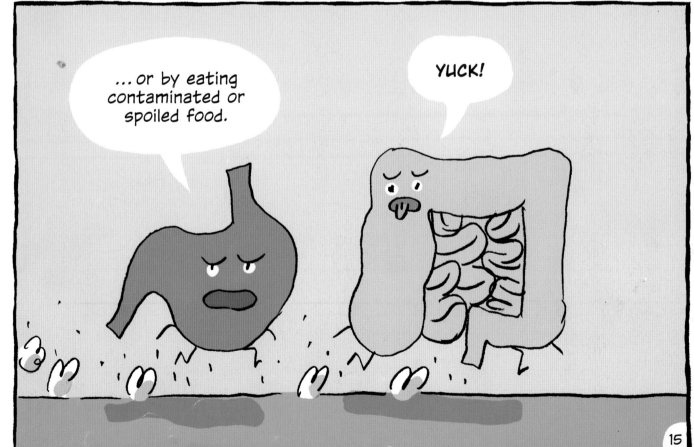

Bacteria are simple organisms made of single cells.

Like me.

Like other organisms, bacteria eat, interact with their environment, make waste, and reproduce.

But when germs infect your body, they leach energy that would otherwise go to building new cells.

Bacteria reproduce by doubling.

If left unchecked, we can wreak havoc!

That's because when some germs use energy, they release harmful substances known as toxins.

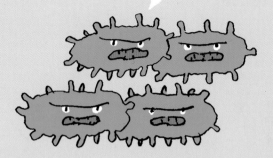

These toxins can destroy your cells...

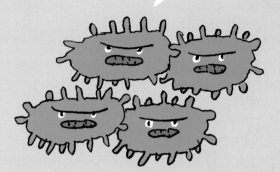

...damage your tissues...

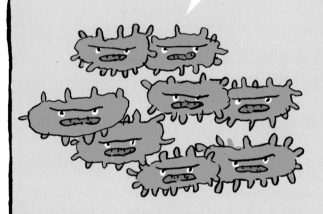

...and disrupt **organ** functions.

Over time, the toxins created by millions of doubling bacteria can cause illnesses, such as pneumonia, food poisoning, and whooping cough.

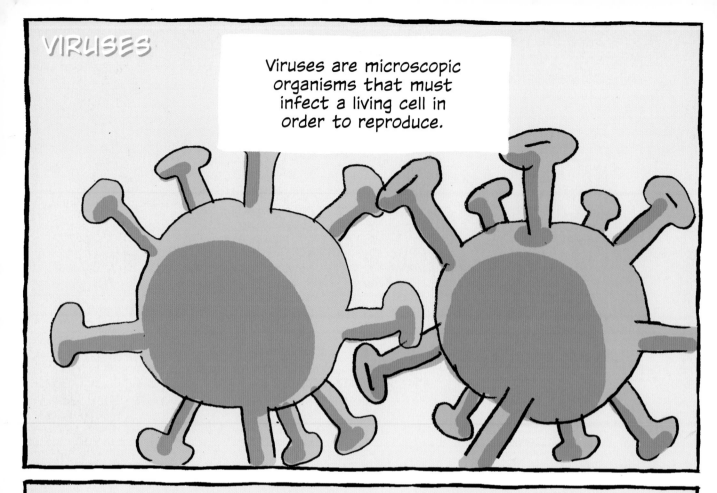

VIRUSES

Viruses are microscopic organisms that must infect a living cell in order to reproduce.

Viruses aren't made of cells, but they are built out of similar stuff.

They usually consist of a handful of genes surrounded by a coat of proteins.

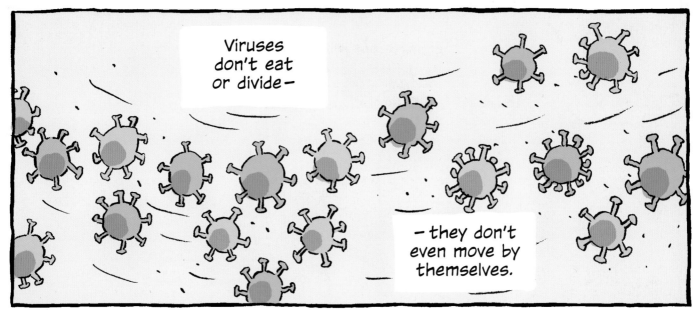

Viruses don't eat or divide—

— they don't even move by themselves.

Because of this, scientists do not consider viruses living things.

Yet, viruses have "survived" on Earth for millions of years.

Whhsshh

Viruses can invade plant cells, animal cells...

...and even other microbes, like bacteria.

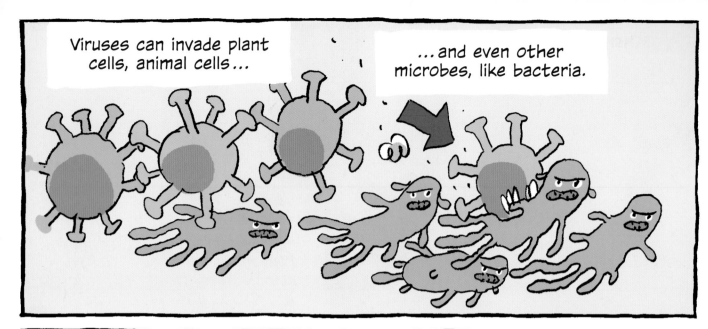

If left unchecked, certain viruses will use your body and its **organ systems** to their advantage.

And because they are so tiny and durable, viruses can be found all around the planet...

...just waiting for an unsuspecting organism.

When a virus enters your body...

...you don't feel sick right away.

PICK PICK

In fact, if your body is healthy, you may not even feel sick at all.

Remember, a virus can't do anything by itself.

And it won't.

A virus needs the cells of your body to do the work for it.

HIJACKING A CELL

The cells in your body have a protective covering.

The **cell membrane** acts like a security system by only admitting particles with the correct chemical combination.

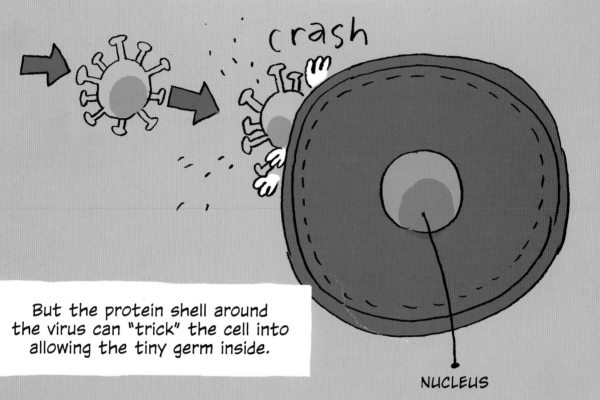

crash

But the protein shell around the virus can "trick" the cell into allowing the tiny germ inside.

NUCLEUS

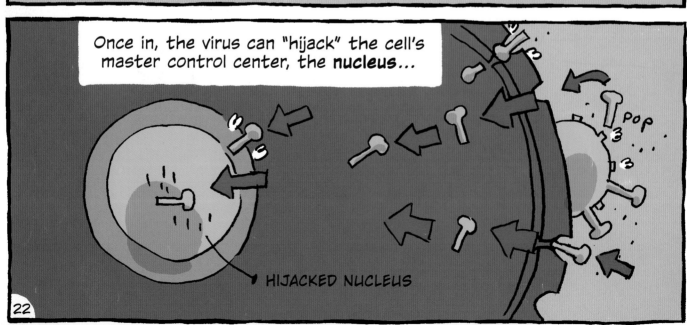

Once in, the virus can "hijack" the cell's master control center, the **nucleus**...

POP

HIJACKED NUCLEUS

...and turn the cell into a virus factory.

Eventually, a swarm of new viruses bursts out of the dying cell and into your body.

crash

If given the chance, the new viruses will continue to infect other cells.

But while the cell is being consumed from inside, your immune system is already preparing a counterattack.

HOLD ON.

I sense a disturbance.

THE IMMUNE RESPONSE

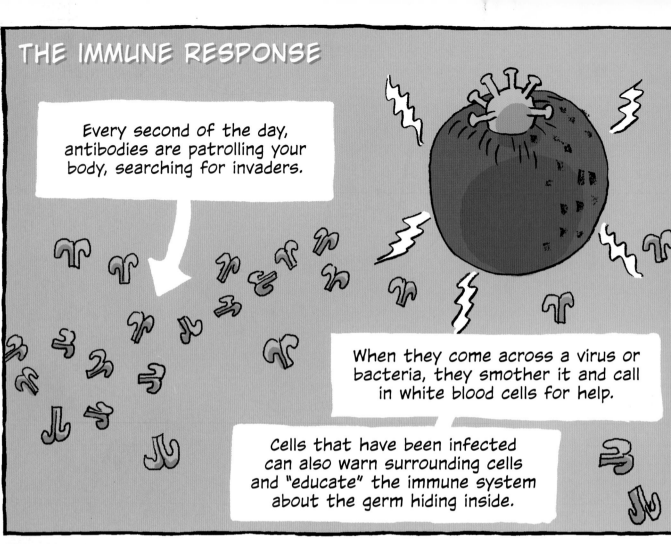

Every second of the day, antibodies are patrolling your body, searching for invaders.

When they come across a virus or bacteria, they smother it and call in white blood cells for help.

Cells that have been infected can also warn surrounding cells and "educate" the immune system about the germ hiding inside.

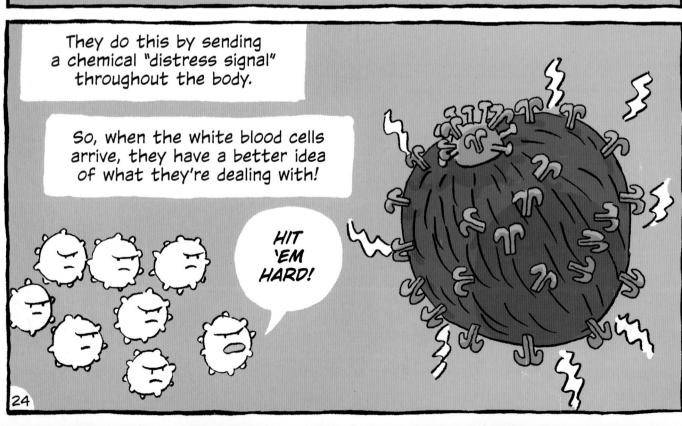

They do this by sending a chemical "distress signal" throughout the body.

So, when the white blood cells arrive, they have a better idea of what they're dealing with!

HIT 'EM HARD!

The white blood cells then produce antibodies that hunt the specific invader.

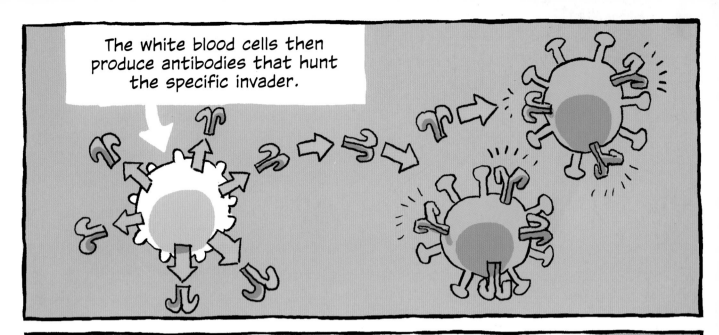

Then the next time your white blood cells encounter this invader, they can kill it before it makes you sick.

munch munch

nom nom

When your immune system identifies an invader once, it remembers.

This is called **immunity!**

BURP!

Beep

Fatigue, fever, and swelling are caused by your immune system fighting an infection.

In fact, many symptoms of "sickness" are caused by the body's defense against an invasion.

However, sometimes microbes can overwhelm the body's defenses.

So, throughout history, doctors and scientists have found new and better ways to fight infection and disease.

Snap

Antibiotics are drugs that can stop a bacterial infection.

These chemicals kill bacteria, but they don't harm viruses.

One way to help your body fight viral infections is called a **vaccine**.

A vaccine is a solution that contains weakened or dead viruses.

Squirt

Poke

ouch

These disabled viruses can't harm your body.

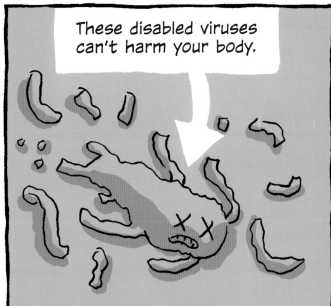

They can, however, train your antibodies and white blood cells to build up an immunity to the virus before it has the chance to make you sick.

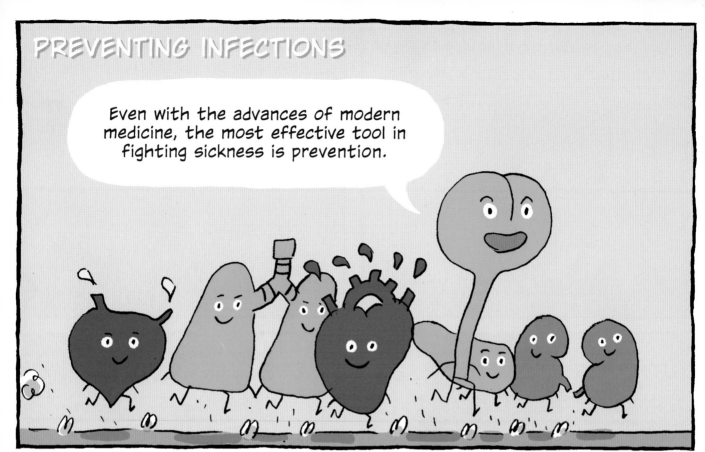

Even with the advances of modern medicine, the most effective tool in fighting sickness is prevention.

Wash your hands often, with soapy water for at least 20 seconds.

That's about how long it takes to sing the ABCs out loud!

28

If you have to cough or sneeze and can't find a tissue, use the inside of your elbow to shield the blast.

HACHOO!

Thank you!

And, a good diet, along with a daily dose of exercise, can help to keep your immune system healthy.

These simple practices can go a long way to prevent the spread of infectious diseases...

...and help your immune system keep germs on the run!

ZIP

ZOOM

GLOSSARY

algae a group of simple organisms that can make their own food. Algae contain chlorophyll but lack true stems, roots, or leaves.

antibiotics useful medications for treating infections caused by bacteria.

antibody a protein that helps other immune cells locate and destroy germs.

bacterium; bacteria a tiny single-celled organism; more than one bacterium.

blood vessels a hollow tube that carries blood and nutrients through the body.

cell the basic unit of all living things.

cell membrane a covering that separates the inside of a cell from the outside environment.

contaminated polluted; made impure.

digestive system the group of organs that breaks down and absorbs food in the body.

disease a disorder of the body or mind.

fungus; fungi any of a group of organisms, such as mushrooms, yeasts, and molds, that produce spores and get nourishment from dead or living matter in nature; the plural of fungus.

immune system the group of organs that protects the body against harmful invaders.

immunity the body's ability to keep out diseases.

infection a disease that can be spread from one person to another.

infectious disease see infection.

microbe a tiny organism, such as a bacterium or virus, that can cause disease.

nucleus the "control center" of a cell.

organ two or more tissues that work together to do a certain job.

organ system two or more organs that do a common task.

orifice an opening in the body.

vaccine a solution of weakened or dead viruses injected into the body that helps to protect against infections before they start.

vector an organism that transmits diseases.

virus a tiny substance that causes certain infections.

white blood cell a cell that helps protect the body against diseases.

FIND OUT MORE

Books

Body Warriors: The Immune System
by Lisa Trumbauer
(Heinemann-Raintree, 2006)

Daring Cell Defenders
by Rebecca L. Johnson
(Millbrook Press, 2007)

Germ Zappers
by Fran Balkwill
(Cold Spring Harbor Laboratory Press, 2001)

Human Body
by Richard Walker
(DK Children, 2009)

Human Body Factory: The Nuts and Bolts of Your Insides
by Dan Green
(Kingfisher, 2012)

Immune System
by Lorrie Klosterman
(Marshall Cavendish Children's Books, 2008)

Start Exploring: Gray's Anatomy: A Fact-Filled Coloring Book
by Freddy Stark
(Running Press Kids, 2011)

The Human Body
by Seymour Simon
(HarperCollins, 2008)

The Immune System
by Susie Derkins
(Rosen Central, 2001)

The Way We Work
by David Macaulay
(Houghton Mifflin/Walter Lorraine Books, 2008)

Websites

Biology 4 Kids: Immune System
http://www.biology4kids.com/files/systems_immune.html
Get an in-depth education on all of the parts that make up the immune system.

E-Learning for Kids: The Immune System
http://www.e-learningforkids.org/Courses/Liquid_Animation/Body_Parts/Immune_System/
Take a peek inside your immune system in this clickable lesson with bonus comprehension exercises.

Kids Health: How the Body Works
http://kidshealth.org/kid/htbw/
Select a body part to watch a video, play a word find, or read an article to learn more about its function in the human body.

Kids.Net.Au: Immune System
http://encyclopedia.kids.net.au/page/im/Immune_system
All of your questions about the immune system will be answered in this description of one of your body systems.

Nobel Prize: Immune System Defender
http://www.nobelprize.org/educational/medicine/immunity/game/index.html
Join the ranks of Immune System Defense Forces as you train to protect your body from invaders!

PBS Science Games: Super Duper Antibodies!
http://pbskids.org/sid/germs.html
Interact with a fun character to learn more about how antibodies help fight sickness in your body.

INDEX